Going Home Married

How to Plan a Meaningful Wedding
Without Losing Your Mind

by Suzyn Jackson Gonzalez

ISBN-13: 978-1469937373
ISBN-10: 1469937379

Cover and interior design by Suzyn Jackson Gonzalez
Author photo by Alvaro J. Gonzalez
Cover image (tree) by Sergey Chernov via istockphoto.com

This book is dedicated to Alvaro,
whose faith in me and
in this book has never wavered.

Contents

Preface

This year, my husband and I will celebrate our tenth wedding anniversary. At this point, my memories of our wedding are a little hazy. I can still feel the panic in the pit of my stomach when my veil fell apart minutes before the ceremony—and my relief when my mom saved the day with a stapler. I can remember wondering why there was no music—turned out our trumpeter was stuck in traffic. I can see the look on my beloved's face when he first saw me. He looked awfully stern, but he told me later he was trying to "keep it together."

And I clearly recall that as soon as our priest said the words "husband and wife," I started to laugh. I knew, at that moment, that the day was a success, that whatever happened from here on in, we were *going home married.* I felt that the months of effort were fulfilled in that moment, and the rest of the day was celebration.

Was it perfect? No. The curried vegetables had no curry, a third of the guests didn't get their favors, and I had *staples in my veil.* So it was not perfect—but it was wonderful.

A WALK THROUGH THE CHOICES YOU'LL MAKE

Weddings can feel like giant puzzles, as you try to piece together a bazillion little choices and make them play nicely together. If you're also trying to accommodate conflicting demands from friends and family—well, it's no wonder people elope.

So right now I want to take a quick jaunt through all the choices you'll make. This is also the outline of the book.

- ❖ First and foremost is the question of what this wedding means to you and, incidentally, what it may mean to the people around you. I suggest working this out and encapsulating your thoughts into an image or phrase so you don't forget them as you move through the rest of the decisions you'll make. I call this a "**touchstone.**"

- ❖ This leads directly to the **ceremony**. Simply put, without a ceremony, it's not a wedding. It's the heart of the day. It may also dictate the **location** and **date**.

- ❖ Next comes the question of **power**, by which I mean how decisions get made and how stuff gets done. Money is a part of this, but only a part.

- ❖ Then we move to some optionals: **party** and **guests**. Yes, they're optional. If you want them, then there are a whole lot of decisions that come after: What sort of party? Who to invite? Your location and date may shift, too. Either way...

- ❖ You'll need **something to wear**.

- ❖ You'll need to figure out a way to let people know your plans. If there's a party, that means **invitations**. If not, that may mean some delicate **conversations**.

- ❖ The rest is **optional**. The sky is the limit, you get to have fun! But nothing else is changing the fact that you're going home married.

Can you handle that? Of course you can. Let's get started.

Introduction

Doorways are interesting things. A house's doorway is like its face to the world. It can tell you a lot about the people who live inside. Are there flowers in pots? Is the door lipstick red or builder's beige? Is the paint peeling? Does the doorbell work? A doorway also colors your experience as you step inside. The high, pointed arch of a gothic cathedral lifts your eyes upwards, to heaven. The low door of a Wabi Sabi teahouse forces even an emperor to bow his head.

Your wedding is a doorway into your marriage. In a world where many milestones have become all but meaningless, and "coming of age" looks a lot like "moseying along," a wedding marks a massive transition from one mode of life to another. It can be either a huge, stressful distraction, or a meaningful foundation for the life you're building together. I wrote this book to help you quell the stress and dig deep to find your own meaning.

DID I SAY STRESS?

Oh, yes.

Let's take a look at some of the thoughts that may be winging their way through your psyche, whether from magazines, your (well intentioned, of course) friends and family, or your own preconceptions.

Your wedding day must be perfect, and [insert expensive item here] will make it perfect.

Can we talk about perfect for a minute? It's an advertiser's mind game. It doesn't exist. That's the whole meaning of perfection: an unattainable ideal. Unattainable. Hear that? You'll never get there.

Here is what I know: the trickster god *loves* weddings. The forces of the universe that cause mischief and mayhem will be present on your big day. Your wedding will not be perfect. I hope it will be wonderful, magical, and deeply meaningful, but I know it will *not* be perfect.

So embrace this idea now: if you go home married, your wedding was a success.

Your wedding day is the most important day of your life.

Um, how about graduation from law school, or the day you met your partner, or having your first kid, or your sixth kid, or getting to the top of Kilimanjaro, or how about getting born yourself? How is any day *the most* important? We're back in advertising gimmick land. Advertisers love superlatives. Just look at car ads: the *best* fuel mileage, the *most* rugged, the *highest* resale value. Any superlative is a big red flag that you're leaving reality and heading for perfection-ville. Don't go there.

Everyone you invite—and everyone you don't—is going to judge you.

Yeah, well, this one is true. In fact, everyone is judging you all the time. Ok, not *all the time*—only when they're thinking about you. Which is not much of the time at all, since they're spending most of their time worrying about how everyone else is judging them.

I will tell you this: when life gets tough and your marriage is tested—when you're sitting in a doctor's office hearing bad news, when you're trying to decide whether to move across the country for an amazing job, when you can't remember whose turn it is to change the 2am diaper—what people thought of your first dance moves is not going to have much bearing. But the memory of dancing with your partner in joy and celebration might just lift you up.

In short, you've got to decide whether to live your life for them or for you. I know—much easier said than done! If this one is really hard for you (it sure is for me), please go now and google "Brené Brown TED."

Wedding =_____

I want you to write down, quickly, whatever comes to mind when you hear the word "wedding." Here, I'll get you started:

- ❖ Big pouffy white dress
- ❖ Crab canapés
- ❖ Open bar
- ❖ Custom-printed cocktail napkins

Keep going…

Now hear this: your wedding does not have to look like that. Those are preconceptions, and you get to toss the ones you don't like in the garbage. Take a big marker and cross out anything in the list above that doesn't feel right.

IT'S THE CEREMONY, STUPID!

(Sorry, I didn't mean to call you stupid. It's the ceremony, sweetheart!)

Cut to the chase time: You're getting married. You're going to start using words like "my husband" and "my wife" (and yes, you're allowed to giggle the first 18 times you use them.)

You wouldn't know it from reading a wedding magazine, but the process of getting married is pretty simple. You do some legal paperwork (a whole lot less than when you buy a house). You show up at a certain time and place, and you promise to love and respect each other for the rest of your lives. An official-type person declares you married. Boom.

A wedding is simply an event where you get married. The ceremony is *it*. The ceremony is what the day is about. Everything else is secondary—the pageantry, the flowers, the dress, the trimmings. It's all icing on the cake (as it were). It's there to announce, amplify, and celebrate the ceremony. You're forming a lifelong commitment. It's one of the few times you get to mark a major life event in the style of your choosing.

A wedding also has deep spiritual and emotional implications. It is an affair of the heart, mind, body, and wallet. Only you know what you need to *feel* married, emotionally and spiritually.

HOW THIS BOOK CAN HELP

Fine, I can hear you thinking. *That's all very nice but it doesn't help me choose whether to get the bells or the doves printed on my cocktail napkins!*

I get it. You've got a gazillion choices in front of you, each one seems monumentally important, and you're feeling overwhelmed. Ok—big deep breath.

Here's the secret: You've already made the two most important choices: you chose your partner, and the two of you chose to get married. You have one more choice to make, something I call the touchstone, which is really just a way of remembering what this whole wedding thing means to you. Once you've made that third choice, all the rest—the dress and the canapés and the cocktail napkins—will sort of fall into line. You'll make the choices that reflect your touchstone. Easy.

Throughout this book, I try to reduce things to their most basic elements, in order to make them easier to think about. When you can see the skeleton clearly, you are free to think creatively about fleshing it out and adding touches to make the result uniquely your own.

THE LIST

When I was planning my wedding, what I wanted more than anything was a list, a simple list that would tell me, "Here's everything you need to think about, and once you've thought about it all, you're done." I read many wedding books, and they all had a list of some sort. Thing was, every list was a little bit different, and they all, well, they all had stuff that was… a little bit silly, or slightly pretentious, or, at the very least, not necessary. I started to divide the lists into optionals and non-optionals, and once I thought about it that way, I saw that the non-optional list was pretty short. Would you like to see it?

- ❖ A ceremony
- ❖ A place and time for the ceremony
- ❖ An officiant
- ❖ Witnesses
- ❖ Some legal paperwork
- ❖ Something to wear
- ❖ A way to tell everyone what's going on
- ❖ A way to thank everyone who helped or wished you well

Truly, if you've got all that, you've got a wedding.

Guests and a party are optional. They go together, though. If you're going to have guests, you really ought to feed them—anything else is just rude. And a party without guests—that's not much of a party.

So, if you want a party, there are a few more non-optionals:

- ❖ Guest list
- ❖ A way to invite people
- ❖ A place and time for the party
- ❖ A transition from ceremony to party
- ❖ Food
- ❖ Music
- ❖ Fun, however you define it

It's still a pretty short list!!

This is not to say that you can't have all the rest: the stretch limo, the rose bower, the centerpieces and the professional photographer, the rehearsal dinner and the gift registry and the trillion other things that we've convinced ourselves are necessary. You can have them and the tent too, darling, *if that's what you want.* Just know that they're optional. That you're choosing them. That they're not required. And most importantly, know that if something goes wrong with any of the optionals, you're still going home married.

If you remember nothing else from this book, remember this:

If you go home married, your wedding was a success.

If, a month later, you *feel* married, your wedding was a triumph.

How to Use this Book

The rest of this book is a bunch of questions. There are no universally right answers. The point is to get you thinking about your wedding and your marriage.

The order of the questions follows a general logic. But feel free to skip around. All the questions cover the same basic ground: what's going to help you *feel* married? In some cases, the answer may pop easily into your head. In others, you may need time for reflection. At the core of the whole book is the question: what does marriage mean to you?

I recommend that you both actually write your answers in the book. It will help, as things get crazy, to see where your thinking was in calmer days.

Many times I'm going to ask you to close your eyes and imagine your big day. The purpose of these exercises is to get your creative juices flowing and bring your dreams, tastes, and quirks—your selves—into the planning process. Please, don't get hung up on perfectly recreating what you see in your head, because no matter what you see in your head, your wedding is going to be slightly different. For one thing, it's going to be real: paid for, obeying the laws of physics, all that. For another thing, it's going to be a *collaboration* with your partner. There are two of you, and you're in this together.

You'll notice that there are spaces for each of you to write. Yes, it's time to sit down with your beloved and start to spin some wedding fantasies. *This is where it gets interesting.* This is where you notice that you have slightly—or greatly—different ideas. Don't start hyperventilating yet—this is a good thing.

What is your idea of a sweet treat?

Cheesecake? Cupcakes? Popsicles? Banana Split? Cookies?

Donuts　　　　　Raspberries

Hmmm, I wonder if your local donut shop would make jelly donuts with a custom fresh raspberry puree filling...

Tension, juxtaposition, the vibration between disparate elements—all these are essential to the creative process. One of you may naturally take the "project manager" role, but it's important to remember that you are not alone in this, just as you're not going to be alone in your marriage. In fact, planning a wedding is an excellent practice run for being married. Learn to enjoy collaboration; welcome your partner's input.

As with any creative endeavor, you are bound to make mistakes, chase down blind alleys, and change your mind. It is all a part of the creative process.

Every individual is unique. And every relationship is unique. Your wedding should be as unique as you two are. What better time to explore, declare and celebrate what makes the combination of the two of you so fantastic that you want to make it permanent? This wedding is about you two, the bond you share and the love that envelops you. True love is a powerful thing. Let your love shine! Your guests will happily bask in the glow.

The best part? That glow will follow you home... married.

Your Touchstone

A PAUSE BEFORE STARTING

You've been expecting it for years, you were completely taken by surprise, you did the asking yourself—it doesn't matter. You have taken one of the biggest steps of your adult life. Take the time to feel, appreciate, relish, and savor the waves of emotion that are rolling across you right now. Enjoy it—it will pass more quickly than you can imagine.

Resolve not to make any decisions right away. Even if you're getting married next Tuesday, take thirty minutes now to gaze into each others' eyes and let it sink in—this is real!

THE BIG QUESTIONS

Your answers to the following questions are going to form the core of your wedding and, to a degree, your married life.

There's no rush. You don't have to have answers right now. But read the questions. Talk them over with your beloved. There is gold here.

Take the time to contemplate these questions away from distractions. Go for a walk, just the two of you. Talk them over with a counselor, a spiritual advisor, or a trusted friend. Write down anything that comes to mind, or feel free to skip ahead and come back to these questions later. The secret is that every other question in the book is essentially asking the same thing.

What is a wedding?

A gateway to your marriage? A legal hassle? A private exchange between the two of you? A statement to the world (and if so, what are you saying)?

What does marriage mean to you?

Why are you getting married?

How do you feel about all this, right now?

Do any aspects of the wedding and married life scare you?

(Hint: it's ok to be scared.)

How do you want to feel on your wedding day? What mood do you want to evoke?

WEDDING DREAMS

Vision comes before creation. And to really get your creative juices flowing, you've got to get rid of any restrictions. Believe me, there will be time enough for restrictions later, no matter who is paying for this thing. But for now, hold your answers to the big questions in your mind, close your eyes, and just imagine...

Did you daydream about your future wedding when you were a kid or a teenager? What did those dreams look like?

What elements of other ceremonies or events have touched you?

Where and when are you happiest?

What was the best party you've ever been to?

What would your wedding look like if money were no object?

Barefoot on the beach? Skiing to an altar at the foot of a mountain? A Zen Buddhist ceremony in a cave? Dinner for 200 of your closest friends at the finest restaurant in town?

DISTILL THE DREAMS

As you examine your dreams, pay close attention to the details. Details can make the difference between a good event and a great event. The details of your dreams can often point the way to what is really important. A well-chosen detail can evoke a dream when you can't afford the whole thing.

❖ So you dreamed of an extravagant, no-holds-barred party at the Plaza Hotel. Take another look at the dream. What is important to you? The sense of luxury? Having all your friends around?

❖ You dreamed of an antebellum tea party straight out of Gone with the Wind, complete with horses, hoopskirts, and a rose bower. What is important in this dream? The connection to history, perhaps your own family tradition? The connection to nature in the garden? Or maybe you're just feeling a touch overwhelmed, and would like a good excuse to keel over in a swoon!

❖ You dreamed of renting out a Tuscan villa, where you and all your friends could cavort through the vineyard, eating grapes and kissing by the fountain. What can you draw from this dream? The romantic destination? The abundance of laughter?

❖ You dreamed that your two best friends pick you both up in a limo with enormous lattes and chocolate croissants, and you all go down to the courthouse and gossip while you stand in line. Done! That was easy! Write down every morsel of detail, splurge on silk underwear, and go to it.

When you dig out old dreams from under their spiritual moth balls, hold them gently, but not reverently. They went into making you who you are. But it's worth asking whether they are still relevant to the person you've become.

❖ You always dreamed of a huge, lavish wedding. At some slumber party in the fifth grade, you decided that if there isn't a big ol' dress, a chamber orchestra, a tent in the botanical gardens, and guys in bow ties handing out cheese puffs, it just isn't a wedding. But now you're an artist/temp, and you're engaged to a poet/musician/waiter, and you love your life. So maybe a $2000 cake doesn't seem so important now.

❖ When you were thirteen, you dreamed of arriving at the church in a horse-drawn carriage. Maybe that was just part of your thirteen-year-old horse phase. Or maybe it could be a way to make your day truly magical, to connect this event to all the planning and scheming and wishing that took up so much of your growing up years. How often do you get to make a dream come true?

This is an exercise in defining your priorities, such as family, tradition, romance, or independence. These priorities will keep you focused though the thousand and one questions, decisions, and pitfalls that make up planning a wedding.

Go back now to your responses, in both the big question and dreams sections, and read them over. Mark significant details that you want to remember. Now circle words and phrases that jump out at you, that seem to hold the essence of what this is all about for you. Copy them down here:

You may be wondering why we are starting with such a big, over-reaching vision. Shouldn't we be starting with the small stuff, the easy stuff? I can hear that shrill voice of panic in your head: *I've got to pick out bridesmaid's dresses, and call the caterer, and did my co-worker say her hairdresser's niece is a photographer?? Do I really have time to look at the big picture!?!?!*

Listen—when you have an idea of where you're going, it's a lot easier to get there. In project planning, this is called the "desired end state." Call it a goal or a vision: it's something big to aim for. Yes, one big decision can seem scarier than a hundred little ones. But that big decision will get you halfway towards solving all the rest.

YOUR TOUCHSTONE

Finally, find a word, phrase, mantra, or image that captures your ideas and feelings. This is your touchstone. This is what you'll come back to, to ground yourself, as the emotions, expectations, and opinions start flying around. This is the calm center of your wedding storm.

We wanted to keep our big day light and keep the laughter flowing. I also knew that I have a tendency to get stuck in taking everything very seriously. Our touchstone was a perfume ad stuck on the fridge, showing gorgeous Isabella Rossellini throwing back her head in laughter.

A single image may not come to you right away. That's all right. Keep mulling over your big questions and your dreams, and one day you'll be checking out flowers or flipping through a magazine or chatting with your beloved and you'll say "That's it! That's everything we want in a nutshell!"

Your Touchstone

A word, phrase, mantra, or image that captures your ideas and feelings

How will you build a wedding around your touchstone? That's for you to decide. In the following chapters, we'll look at all the individual decisions there are to be made. Keep your touchstone in mind, and the rest will fall into line. Don't get mired in the details, take a lot of deep breaths, and remember how lucky you are to have found this amazing person that you want to spend the rest of your life with.

Ceremony

Second only to the decision of whom you will marry, the choice of vows is of paramount importance. It is the vows that distinguish this day, and this event, from any other party. All the other choices you will make simply form the frame to offset and celebrate the main event—the formation of your marriage.

Therefore, take the utmost care in choosing the vows you will take. These vows are not to be made lightly. They will forever affect the shape and substance of your life.

YOUR SPIRITUAL LIFE

This is a perfect time to share and explore the spiritual contexts in which the two of you were brought up, and where you find yourself now. If you have not yet discussed your current beliefs, and the beliefs with which you were raised, now is the time. How did being raised Catholic affect your understanding of marriage, whether you now practice or not? Do your Buddhist principles mesh with your partner's Jewish faith, and can you find a way to acknowledge both in a marriage ceremony? Are you willing to participate in a full Hindu ceremony, even though neither of you understand Sanskrit? As Agnostics, does the standard civil ceremony encompass everything you want to say to each other, or do you feel the need to write your own vows?

Explore the marriage rites of your and your partner's heritages, and any others to which you feel drawn. Discuss the role of spirituality in your lives. If your marriage is to be a true meeting of hearts and minds, do not shy from bringing your spiritual lives into play.

I would urge you to consider carefully before walking through a ceremony in which you do not believe and speaking words you do not mean, simply for the sake of form or to satisfy family. While it is important to have the blessing and support of your friends and family, it is much, much more important that you feel married in your heart, and that you perform whatever steps it will take for you to do so. Ultimately, this marriage consists of the two of you, and it is your commitment to each other that will make or break it.

In what spiritual context/tradition were you brought up?

What are your current beliefs/practices?

What is your heritage's traditional marriage rite?

Do these rites hold meaning for you?

Do you want to use the traditional rites intact? Are there certain elements that you could incorporate into your ceremony?

Are there any other rites that hold meaning for you?

You don't have to stick with your cultural or spiritual heritage, if it doesn't speak to you.

What will help you to be "in the moment" for your ceremony?

Many elements of traditional rites serve to bring us fully into the moment: ringing of bells, lighting of candles, singing, prayer.

Whether you choose to follow a tradition or create your own ritual, there are a few elements common to all weddings. Thinking about this framework and how you would like to interpret it will help to open a door into thinking about the deeper significance of the events of the day.

Plan your day so that you can be calm, present and aware during the ceremony. Listen to the words, and look people in the eye. This is what life is all about. This is the good stuff.

THE ENTRANCE

How do you want to arrive?

Separately? Together? Escorted? By whom? Before or after your guests assemble?

Do you want close family or friends by your side? Why?

Also knows as best man, maid of honor, ushers, bridesmaids, flower girls, and ring bearers.

Do you want to arrive silently, or to music?

What sort of music?

What atmosphere do you want to create as you step, single, into the space that you will leave married?

What do you want to carry?

Flowers, candles, a bell, a hankie?

Do you want to meet your partner before the event or during?

Will you stay apart the night before and the day of the wedding? Will you have breakfast together to savor the day, and then help each other dress? Will you see each other for the first time through a crowd of everyone you care about, all dressed up and looking swell?

THE VOWS

Most wedding vows are pretty simple, at their heart. You promise to love and honor each other for the rest of your lives, and to live within the bonds of marriage. All the other words and deeds—the prayers, the questions, the rings, the songs and readings—serve to signify and amplify the importance of these vows, to set them apart from everyday life, and to flavor the entity that is being formed, the family, the "corporate unit" as our priest called it, the marriage.

Words and actions have power, and all the preparation, thought, attention, and sweat that you have put into the simple words and actions of a wedding ceremony only serve to lend them more power. Consider carefully the words that will be spoken, and the actions that will be performed. This is the birth of your marriage. How do you want it to begin?

What promise do you intend to make to your partner?

What promise do you want to receive from your partner?

Do the traditional vows from your heritage cover what you want to say and hear?

What words do you want to speak on your wedding day?

Given all your other answers, do you want to write your own vows?

OFFICIANT

If the choice of spiritual tradition seems vague and nebulous, the choice of officiant is very specific. Someone has to pronounce you husband and wife, and that person will often set the tone of the ceremony. Two different people even within the same denomination can put a wildly different spin on the event, and so it is important to select someone that you like, who takes the time to understand who you are and what this wedding means to you. In many religious traditions, this person may act as a spiritual advisor during the course of your engagement. Do not hesitate to ask questions, discuss thorny issues, and trust your gut when it comes to this decision.

You may already know a priest, rabbi, or judge, that you assumed would officiate at your wedding. Are you both happy with this choice? If not, consider...

What qualities do you want in an officiant?

What questions do you want to ask potential officiants when you meet them?

Who will marry you?

RINGS

The flowers will fade, the dress will be packed away, and the cake will turn to an inedible lump in your freezer, but your wedding ring will stay with you for the length of your marriage. You may develop nervous ticks, checking to make sure it is still there. Every time you look at it, you will be reminded of your wedding day, and of the partner you love so well. Choose thoughtfully.

Will you exchange rings or other symbols of your commitment? What do the rings or talismans mean to you?

THE REST

Are there other elements—readings, songs, a religious or spiritual exercise—that you want to include?

Do you want friends and family to participate?

If so, who? What are you looking for them to contribute to the moment?

Will you have "audience participation"? If so, how will you help people follow along?

A program? An order of service? A master of ceremonies?

THE EXIT

Before you know it, it will all be over, you'll be married, and you'll leave for the party.

How do you want to leave the space where you got married?

A trumpet fanfare? A thousand bubbles?

How do you want to make your first progress together as a married unit? Where will go you from here?

The ceremony *is* the wedding, the core of your big day. In the chapters that follow, we'll explore ways to expand on that core, celebrate and elevate it, so that it feels just as special as it really is.

$\mathcal{P}ower$

Wait—a discussion of power in a wedding book? Fear not: I'm not going to recommend raw eggs or even a single bench press. What I mean by power is simply how decisions get made and how things get done.

Sad to say, weddings are ripe for power struggles. I've seen some doozies just amongst my friends and family. Weddings have a way of drawing out any latent conflicts, either between you as a couple, or within your families—even ones you didn't realize were there! So, what can you do about this? Well, just being aware of it is helpful. Better, though, to meet it head-on with firm decisions and respectful conversations. (Hint: this is also good practice for, you know, *life*.) Nothing can suck the joy out of a wedding faster than angst and drama, and putting your fingers in your ears and singing "La! La! La!" does not make them go away.

MONEY

Money questions *seem* simple—after all, they deal with figures and they should have simple mathematical answers—but usually they are anything but.

Why? Because money is power made visible.

- ❖ Where you spend your money is concrete evidence of your priorities. So it's important to sort out your priorities before you spend a dime. That's what the touchstone chapter is about.

- ❖ Whoever is supplying the money generally has a big say in how it gets spent. The question becomes: who do you want calling the shots?

My husband and I chose to pay for our own wedding, and I think it was one of the best decisions we made. It didn't make for a smooth and easy road. Time and again, we found that we couldn't afford our first impulses. We would dream something up, do the research, price it, recover from the sticker shock, and then sit back down at the drawing board. We relegated those initial dreams to the "awesome 25th anniversary party we're going to throw when we have tons of money" file. Then we went back to our touchstone and started again. In the end, we spent a fair amount of time paying off the credit cards; but ultimately every decision was our own. Our relationship was strengthened and deepened by working together on such a large project, and we had a lot of fun in the process.

In hindsight, I believe that the challenge of having to think creatively about our wedding brought out much better end results than had we simply been able to fork over the cash for our first ideas. Even if we had had triple the budget, I don't think we would have had a better time, or a more beautiful wedding.

Your situation may be different. You may be in a position to receive much needed help from your families. I'm not saying that's a bad thing. I just want you to be conscious of what you're exchanging for that financial help: families plus money make a ripe ground for drama. Think it through, and talk it through—both together and with your families—well ahead of time.

As you sit down to consider your budget, keep in mind all your other priorities in life. These may include schooling, housing, travel, starting a business, or having kids. Diapers are expensive! Make sure that you're spending your resources in a way that reflects who you are, what you value, and where you are headed in life.

Compounding these complexities is the fact that the moment you put the word "wedding" in front of *anything*, the price goes up. A flower arrangement costs X, but *wedding* flowers cost more. A dress costs X, but a *wedding* dress can cost several times that. (By the way, the opposite is true for honeymoons. For some reason, people love throwing freebies at honeymooners.) Fitting your wedding dreams into your wedding budget is a great exercise in creative thinking.

What are your priorities—for the wedding, and in life?

Who's paying for this thing?

Is there more than one source?

How are you going to handle decision-making?

If there's more than one source, how will responsibilities—and choices—be divided?

What's your budget?

This is not a detailed budget, not yet. Right now, just agree on a number—the total amount that you can reasonably afford to spend. Agree not to go above this number.

As you start pricing out all the various parts of your wedding, keep a simple tally. If you go above your agreed budget, it's time to tweak something. The advantage of the work you're doing throughout this book is that you can easily see whether your spending is lining up with your priorities. Spend on the stuff that matters to you, and be a scrooge on the rest.

Magazines: A Word of Caution

Your first instinct may be to buy an armload of wedding magazines for "inspiration." Fine, just keep in mind that these magazines exist first and foremost to sell ad space. The advertisers' agenda is to get you to spend as much money on your wedding as possible. They use every psychological trick in the book to get you anxious, confused, and eager to spend. So go ahead and buy the pretty magazines, but take what they have to say with a grain—or a shovel-full—of salt.

Remember, it is a wedding, not a popularity contest. People who love you will respect you for putting on the best party you can, *within your means.* On the other hand, it's important to focus on your priorities, not on economizing every step of the way. Don't nickel and dime yourself out of having a beautiful wedding, a wonderful time, and creating fabulous memories.

It's a ceremony—which doesn't need to cost much at all—plus a party, which can cost anywhere from zero to several million bucks (and that's not including the honeymoon!) Whatever your budget, you're going home married.

HELP

Regardless of your budget, weddings tend to be a lot of work. Some people—me, for example—are terrible at asking for help. Whether it is independence or perfectionism or ego, we tend to think that we have to do it all. Well, now is a good time to learn to ask for help. I don't want you to be sick or exhausted on your wedding day.

Here's what I learned: most people *like to help*, and being asked—graciously—for their help makes them feel special and acknowledged. The trick is to ask, not demand, and to give great heaping loads of thank yous. In fact, I believe that help is just as deserving of a formal thank you note as a silver-plated cake server.

Now, chances are that a great deal of your helpers will be family. This could be a boon or a drag, depending on your family, or even depending on each individual family member.

No one knows your family as well as you do. Decide who will work with which family members. Enlist the help of the family diplomat, on both sides. It is not your job to make everyone happy at the expense of your own sanity. However, a few happy family members can make life a lot easier.

Remember, also, that family members have wedding dreams, too! Some parents start imagining their kid's wedding when said kid is still in utero. Talk to your families about their wedding dreams. Your touchstone comes from the two of you, but you may choose to incorporate at least some of the priorities, expectations, and preferences of your families.

Who could help? | **With what?**

Who could help?

With what?

Who will expect (insist, demand) to be involved?

Can you find a role for them?

Vital Conversations

Plan to talk with close family members on both sides, to discuss dreams, wishes, and expectations. Remember that listening is just as important as talking—maybe even more so.

Meeting #1

Who do you need to meet with?

What do you need to ask? Say?

What did they say?

Were you able to come to any agreement?

Meeting #2

Who do you need to meet with?

What do you need to ask? Say?

What did they say?

Were you able to come to any agreement?

Meeting #3

Who do you need to meet with?

What do you need to ask? Say?

What did they say?

Were you able to come to any agreement?

BEYOND MOOLAH: YOUR TALENTS

You've got more going for you than your bank balance. Chances are what you're good at corresponds to what is important to you. When couples get creative, the effects are powerful, charming, and wonderfully unique. Being surrounded by things that you made, or that were made for you, creates a magic that no "wedding expert" can replace.

What are your talents? What are you really good at?

Can you bake a mean cake? Embroider or paint a banner? Build a bower? Sing a love song?

How can you incorporate your talents into your wedding?

What about your family and friends? Can you invite their creativity into the mix? Consider the skills and obsessions of your helpers. You may not know a crocus from a chrysanthemum, but it could make your aunt's year to do your flowers. A buddy with a van is invaluable in shleppling wedding stuff. Does your sister-in-law excel at telling people what to do? Make her the major domo, the person who makes sure things go according to plan on the big day. We were lucky enough to have several talented amateur photographers with high-end digital cameras at our wedding—we didn't hire a photographer, and our albums are gorgeous.

This is not about saving money. This is about adding meaning for you and your helpers.

How can you incorporate your family and friends' talents into your wedding?

However you end up paying for your wedding, take the time now to set some guidelines for how decisions will be made. Then explain to everyone involved how you want to handle this, and let them air their feelings. Respect that anyone who is contributing time or money should have a say in the proceedings, but don't lose sight that it is *your* wedding. You may have to do a delicate balancing act between letting go of a certain amount of control and accepting much needed help.

Par-tay

TO PARTY OR NOT TO PARTY?

It needs to be said: the party part of a wedding is optional.

If you just snorted, then obviously it's not optional to you. And I do believe there is a deep-seated human need to celebrate, dance, and eat when something big happens.

But let's step back for a second. Many of the rigidly codified rules that you'll encounter around weddings have to do with the party. It can seem as if your only choices are: sit-down or buffet? Open bar or signature aperitifs? Speeches between courses or after dinner? Groom's cake? Little gifties for everyone? Better start practicing for that excruciating first dance!!

All this assumes that the party *is* the wedding, and that's just not true. By the time you get to the party, the vows have been spoken and the deal is done. You're already married. Renting out a hall and hiring a caterer is *one way* to celebrate that fact, but certainly not the only one.

Now, you may decide to go with some of the standard elements: dance with your dad, hire a DJ. Standards are standards for a reason—something about them works. But let's not jump to conclusions too quickly. As I said earlier, the party exists to announce, amplify, and celebrate the ceremony. So let's start with the ceremony.

Go back to your touchstone, and to the vows you intend to make. Let them sit in your mind, in your heart. Now…

Once the vows are spoken and the marriage is sealed, what do you want to do next? How do you want to celebrate?

How do you see the transition from Ceremony to Party?

Separation of church and state (as it were)? Or a graceful flow? One location or two?

Do you want to separate the ceremony and the party completely?

An intimate ceremony followed hours or weeks later by a blow-out party?

GUESTS

If you're *not* having a party, consider carefully whether you want to invite people. It's totally fine not to have a party, but to invite people and then not feed them? In my opinion that's rude.

However, I strongly believe that it is far more important to invite everyone you want to attend than to feed everyone filet mignon. It may feel at times like you have to impress everybody, but for the most part, people just want to wish you well and celebrate your happiness. The essence of etiquette is making everyone comfortable, not spending X number of dollars per head. Matter of fact, some of the best parties I've ever been to were potlucks—just sayin'!

What this means is: draw up your guest list *completely independent* of your budget. Then, when you have the two in place, you can figure out how they fit together. Remember, too, that there is no magical right number of guests. Invite the people you want to be there—that's your right number.

Have you got your touchstone firmly in mind? Yes, that absolutely applies to whom you choose to invite.

Do you want guests?
Is this a public or a private affair? Would guests add to the meaning of the day?

If you do want guests, what are you hoping they will add to the event? In other words, why do you want them there?

Blessings? Support? Witness? A party atmosphere?

Considering everyone you know, who is likely to bring that?

This is the core of your guest list.

Are there other people that you feel you _have_ to invite?

If these people may detract from the day, what can you do to head off the worst-case scenario?

This could be anything from a candid conversation beforehand, to deciding not to serve alcohol, to asking a cousin to keep an eye on your crotchety great-uncle.

Take heart—if you create an atmosphere of love and respect, most people will bring their best selves. And it's not going to be perfect anyway, remember?

Finally, looking over your guest list, consider whether you'll need to make any special accommodations for anyone.

Are there people on your list who...

- ❖ Have difficulty walking?
- ❖ Have difficulty standing for long periods of time?
- ❖ Might have trouble walking over uneven ground, or up flights of stairs?
- ❖ Are particularly sensitive to heat or cold?
- ❖ Have allergies to food or fragrance?
- ❖ Are kids? (Ask a parent to help plan kid-friendly activities and accommodations)
- ❖ Need any special care or consideration?

The essence of etiquette is making your guests feel comfortable. Anticipating your guests' needs is a loving and respectful thing to do.

AMBIANCE

Ambiance has everything to do with a great party. Get your guests (and yourself) in the mood and you're halfway there. Your touchstone is all about atmosphere, mood—emotions.

So let's go back to your touchstone and delve into the mood you want to evoke.

What kind of mood does your touchstone suggest?

A solemn, formal affair? A joyous romp? A casual party? A quiet, intimate celebration?

Now it's time for some ambiance reconnaissance! Go to places that evoke your mood, and notice the details. Does your favorite cozy restaurant have low lighting, lots of red and brown, and mellow jazz playing? Does the hotel lobby that lifts your spirits have crystal chandeliers, gold accents, sparkling light everywhere, and Vivaldi piped in? Look at lighting, color, proportions of space, volume and type of music—all the elements that create atmosphere. Try to identify the factors that make up the atmosphere you love, so that you can re-create them for your event.

Location #1

What is the mood here?

What is the lighting like?

How big is the space?

What is the temperature?

Is there music? What type?

What colors do you see?

How many people are around? Is it crowded?

Note the little details:

Circle anything you want to reproduce.

Location #2

What is the mood here?

What is the lighting like?

How big is the space?

What is the temperature?

Is there music? What type?

What colors do you see?

How many people are around? Is it crowded?

Note the little details:

Circle anything you want to reproduce.

Location# 3

What is the mood here?

What is the lighting like?

How big is the space?

What is the temperature?

Is there music? What type?

What colors do you see?

How many people are around? Is it crowded?

Note the little details:

Circle anything you want to reproduce.

By paying attention to details and focusing on a mood, you'll end up with something more than "generic wedding." You'll have a gorgeous event that says "you."

ACTIVITIES

Once you've got your ambiance firmly in mind, let's think about what you and your guests are going to *do* during this party, and plan a time and a place to do it all. I also recommend thinking about your music in relation to activities—you may want very different music for cocktails than for dancing. One of my biggest pet peeves with weddings is when the DJ takes over and plays music so loudly that conversation becomes impossible. So please, plan in a zone for those who really do want to hear all about Aunt Rhonda's trip to Thailand.

Write down every activity you want to include, from drawing your names on the night sky with sparklers to games for the flower girls and ushers.

Activity	Location / Time	Music

Activity	Location / Time	Music

DÉCOR

Your ambiance reconnaissance should have given you lots of great ideas for décor. When decorating a space, the most effective ideas are bold, simple, and consistent. They don't need to be expensive. Use your imagination, and remember that it only has to last for one night.

When you close your eyes and imagine your wedding, what details do you see?

Piles of candles, of every height and shape? Roses everywhere? Picnic tables with big galvanized tubs of daisies? Banners fluttering? Bonfires on the beach?

What are your favorite colors? Paste samples here.

Consistent use of color is one of the strongest and cheapest visual statements you can make.

What areas of your location will get the most exposure?

Concentrate on the places that will be seen by the most people, for the most time.

FOOD AND DRINK

I can't remember how many times, in the excitement of getting dressed for an afternoon wedding, I've forgotten to eat lunch. Wedding guests aren't all that different than toddlers: we get cranky when we're hungry. So whatever you feed people, feed 'em *plenty*, *early* and *often*.

What is your favorite meal?

Yes, you can have a morning wedding and feed everyone pancakes.

What sort of meal do your touchstone and ambiance suggest?

A formal meal or finger food?

On the practical side, what can you afford to serve?

Where does your budget fall on the peanuts-to-filet mignon spectrum?

Where can you find your favorite food?

A caterer isn't your only option; consider restaurants, gourmet food shops, your kitchen, even warehouse stores for those frozen mini-quiches!

How do you feel about serving alcohol?

You guessed it: alcohol is optional!

What is your favorite drink?

Consider keeping things simple and offering only a few choices.

What is your idea of a sweet treat?

Cheesecake? Cupcakes? Popsicles? Banana Split? Cookies?

❖ Going Home Married

The party is the fun part, because the ceremony is over and you're already married. Every single part of the party could go wrong, and you'll still be married!! So please focus on enjoying time with your loved ones and savoring the awesome emotions of the day.

Location and Date

As a simple matter of physics, your wedding ceremony will have to occur at a fixed place and time, and these things will affect your ceremony deeply. An early morning wedding mass at the cathedral will feel very different than a simple sunset ceremony on the beach. Likewise, before you choose the place and time, it's important to decide *whether or not you want a party,* and what kind of party you want. Take a good look through both the ceremony and the party chapters before you commit to a location or place. However, you won't be able to fully complete your ceremony or party plans until you decide on a date and place.

As you begin to think about locations, consider whether you want to set your wedding within or apart from your everyday life. Do you want to get married in the place where you've chosen to live? Do want to return to the place where you grew up to form your family of two? Or do you want to differentiate your wedding as much as possible from your day-to-day life?

First things first…

Do your ceremony plans require a particular location?

Is it important that you get married in the church you attended as a child, or could it be any church? Are you firmly set on getting married on the beach where you met, or could it be any outdoor location?

Do your ceremony plans requires a particular time of day/year?

Do you need a Beltane feast? Advent blessings? Cherry blossoms? Sunrise?

It's time to close your eyes, again. (Ok, read this paragraph, *then* close your eyes!) Think of your touchstone. It's alright if you don't have a crystal-clear picture of your wedding yet, but imagine the mood of the day. Now try to zero in on a particular detail. It could be a song you know you want to play, the trim of your dress, a look you're hoping to see on someone's face. Got it? Now, as if you were a cinematographer, zoom out to a wider shot.

Where are you?

What is significant to you about that spot?

What season is it? Is it a special time of day or year for you?

Is it at all practical—or even possible—to hold your wedding where and when you are imagining?

If not, is there something about that place and time that you can include in your event?

LOGISTICS

These are the practicalities of "getting to the church on time."

What city or general area are you planning on?

Can you get to it easily?

Are you willing to undertake long-distance event planning? Could someone there help you?

Will most of your guest list be able and willing to travel there?

Is Mother Nature likely to interfere?

The best-laid schemes of mice and men are no match for a seasonal blizzard.

BRAINSTORM

Still struggling to come up with an idea? Here are some possibilities.

- ❖ House of Worship, adjoining hall
- ❖ Courthouse (after the parking tickets and before the indecent exposure case) or Judge's chambers
- ❖ Public Space: park, square, museum, landmark (plan on a few strangers attending!)
- ❖ Private Space: a home, barn, cabin, or back yard
- ❖ Restaurant
- ❖ Hotel, Inn, or "Event Space"
- ❖ Destination: usually a far-off resort
- ❖ Gallery, Museum
- ❖ Zoo—why not?
- ❖ The place where you met
- ❖ Adventure: snorkeling, skydiving, Las Vegas
- ❖ Flash mob at the mall?

Does anything in my list pique your interest? If not, just keep writing. Write down anything you can think of. The key to a brainstorm is not to question anything while you're in the writing stage. Something in your list will work for you.

SITE VISITS

We've been doing a lot of dreaming. Now let's invite reality to the party. It's time to visit a few places and pick one. I've included a list of practical questions to ask while you're there, because parties are always more fun when everyone is comfortable. You don't have to answer yes to each question—if there's no place to sit, you can always bring in chairs—but your answers will give you some ideas of how you'll need to work with the space.

Location #1

Will your officiant work here?

Is there enough room for everyone you want to invite?

Is there a place for people to sit down, if they need to?

Is there adequate shade? Shelter? Bathrooms?

Will they provide food, or limit the food and drink you can bring?

Is the space set up for food, music, dancing... all the elements you want to incorporate? Will you need elaborate set up (and break-down)?

Is the space available on a date that works for you?

Have you read all paperwork carefully?
Public spaces usually require permits, and private spaces can require elaborate contracts.

Can you see yourself celebrating here?

Location #2

Will your officiant work here?

Is there enough room for everyone you want to invite?

Is there a place for people to sit down, if they need to?

Is there adequate shade? Shelter? Bathrooms?

Will they provide food, or limit the food and drink you can bring?

Is the space set up for food, music, dancing... all the elements you want to incorporate? Will you need elaborate set up (and break-down)?

Is the space available on a date that works for you?

Have you read all paperwork carefully?
Public spaces usually require permits, and private spaces can require elaborate contracts.

Can you see yourself celebrating here?

Location #3

Will your officiant work here?

Is there enough room for everyone you want to invite?

Is there a place for people to sit down, if they need to?

Is there adequate shade? Shelter? Bathrooms?

Will they provide food, or limit the food and drink you can bring?

Is the space set up for food, music, dancing... all the elements you want to incorporate? Will you need elaborate set up (and break-down)?

Is the space available on a date that works for you?

Have you read all paperwork carefully?
Public spaces usually require permits, and private spaces can require elaborate contracts.

Can you see yourself celebrating here?

Location #4

Will your officiant work here?

Is there enough room for everyone you want to invite?

Is there a place for people to sit down, if they need to?

Is there adequate shade? Shelter? Bathrooms?

Will they provide food, or limit the food and drink you can bring?

Is the space set up for food, music, dancing... all the elements you want to incorporate? Will you need elaborate set up (and break-down)?

Is the space available on a date that works for you?

Have you read all paperwork carefully?
Public spaces usually require permits, and private spaces can require elaborate contracts.

Can you see yourself celebrating here?

You can get married practically anywhere! So have fun picking a lovely spot, some place that will be conducive to your and your guest's comfort. And remember that this spot will become endowed with meaning for you, even if it has none right now. My husband and I try to visit our little spot in Central Park on every anniversary! But most of all, don't sweat this decision. Remember that the choice of *where* you do it is far less important than *what* you're going to do there.

Clothes

If a party is optional, well, clothes are not. Unless you're a nudist, you've got to wear *something*! Now, I'm about to distort the space-time continuum of the wedding universe by addressing menswear and womenswear *at the same time*. Watch out.

As I see it, your clothing—be it a gown, a tux, or a sarong—has three tasks to accomplish:

❖ Reflect your touchstone, be part of the ambiance of the day

❖ Let you be comfortable

❖ Make you look fantastic

It's a tall order, but I believe it can be done. I do NOT subscribe to the notion of suffering for fashion! In addition to having wonderful pictures, I want you to have wonderful memories. It's going to be a long day, you'll probably spend most of it on your feet, and you owe it to yourself not to have to worry about or be encumbered by your clothing. I'll let you in on a secret—with the possible exception of your lucky sweats, the more comfortable you are, the sexier you are. And sexy (the subtle, comfortable kind) is a great thing to be on your wedding day

THE LOOK OF LOVE

Step one. Let go of all notions of "what people wear to get married." Close you eyes and go back over everything you've dreamed or decided so far: your touchstone, your ceremony, the party afterwards, the mood and emotions you want to evoke. Now, how would you translate all of that into clothing?

What overall style are you going for?

Formal, casual, sporty? Sophisticated? Rustic? Beachy?

It's totally fine to look through magazines and browse online for inspiration images at this stage. In fact, it might help you sort out ideas with a partner who has no idea what "preppy" means. Don't limit yourself to "bridal" sources either—as you did with your touchstone, look anywhere and everywhere. Even if you decide to keep your final outfits a secret, it's helpful to agree on an overall look to start with.

Remember, though, that this is only the first step. Images won't tell you what the clothing looks like *on you*. For that you are you to need…

THE SHOPPING TRIP

Now put down the magazines, grab your sister, the friend who always looks great, or anyone else you trust, and go shopping! Comb your hair, do your makeup (if you're so inclined), put on good underwear, and wear something that makes you feel like a million bucks—it'll be a good baseline to come back to. If a style doesn't look better than your favorite outfit, it's not the style for you.

Plan to visit a few places, anywhere that might fit with your style. Don't worry about price point, not yet. The thing is, you're not shopping for your actual clothes at this point. You're looking for shape and color, and keeping an eye out for special details. Don't even look at the price tags. Any shape, and any color, can be reproduced in any price range. (The dress I made cost one tenth the price of the Vera Wang gown I initially fell for).

Try on slinky bias-cut dresses and big pouffy things. Try on strapless numbers and flowy, angelic costumes. Pay attention to how they make you look, and how they make you feel. Do you stand up straighter in this one? Does that one show off your shoulders? Do you have curves you never knew you had? Do you spend all of your time sucking in your stomach in the satin? Do you want to spend your wedding day sucking in your stomach? Does that cut completely eliminate the "figure problem" you always obsess about? Does stark white light you up or make you look like a corpse? Does pale pink make you glow? Does sparkly beading make you smile? Does lace itch?

Do you feel like dancing in a top hat and tails? Do you look like a prince or a waiter in that Nehru jacket? Does a fantastic suit with a fantastic tie make you feel powerful? Does a dinner jacket make you feel like Carey Grant? Does wool itch? Do wide lapels balance your shoulders?

If wearing a Kinte Cloth evokes your African heritage in a meaningful way, by all means wear it. If your Dutch-Irish blood is crying out for a ruby-red Vietnamese Ao Dai, it may be just what you need to set off your pale skin. Smoking jackets, doublet and hose, Kimonos—all these and wilder have been and will be worn at weddings. Let your imagination soar. People have been getting married around the world for millennia. Just because Queen Victoria started a trend by flouting practicality and wearing a white wedding dress doesn't mean you have to.

Don't forget accessories and headgear, too! Haven't you always wanted to know what you would look like with a fascinator attached to your skull!? How about a mantilla, or a veil, or a top hat? Does the choker that looks so appealing peeking out from under a shirt collar look like it's cutting off your head when you're in a bustier? Does a polka-dotted bow tie hint at your fabulous sense of humor? Try on shoes, too—get the full picture. And brave a few makeup counters to play dress-up with your face.

Shopping Notes

What worked	**What didn't**
Shape	
Color	
Texture	
Details	

Shopping Notes

What worked

Shape

Color

Texture

Details

What didn't

THE FINAL DEAL

Now that you've done the reconnaissance work, you should have a better idea of what suits you, how it feels, and what it all looks like.

What are you looking for, specifically?

Once you know what you're looking for, it will be much easier to find it at a price that fits your budget. If you can afford the thing you fell in love with, by all means buy it! If not, it's time to get creative, either through ju-jitsu shopping (after-prom clearance, discount stores, sample sales, vintage, ebay) or by making it yourself. Whichever route you choose, make sure that you give yourself as much time as possible, and enlist the help of a professional tailor or seamstress, as getting the fit "just right" can take much longer than you ever expected.

Even if you opt for store-bought clothes, consider making some small part of your or your partner's outfit—earrings, garter, a sweater, an embroidered pocket poof. There is undoubtedly something powerful about wearing your own creation. Your time and effort (and dare I say love?) are crystallized in the garment, and you are fed by your own work.

Is there any part of your outfit you could make?

Is there a way to incorporate sentimental details?

Buttons from your grandmother's wedding dress? A love note tucked in your pocket?

Finally, try everything on together, including shoes and jewelry. It's very difficult to gauge proportion until you can see everything at once. And if you're willing, check out both outfits together. Now is the time to discover that an angora sweater leaves lint all over a tux, not five minutes before photographs!

How does it look when you put it all together?

Get a few people's opinions.

Name	Opinion

Name   **Opinion**

GORGEOUS YOU

Ultimately, this day is about you, not about your dress or your tie or your shoes. The clothes you wear are simply the packaging that allows you to be the very best you on this day. Think about who you are, at this moment, at your age, embarking on this great adventure. You do not have to be the best you that ever was or ever will be, simply the best you *right now*. How did you get to this point in your life? Where are you going from here? Obviously you're pretty wonderful—after all, someone wants to partner with you for life! Show yourself off. Not your body or your earrings—your *self*. The inner light that makes you unique. Keep the outfit simple, and concentrate on being calm, centered, and present. The glow that will bathe you when you let yourself feel all the feelings of the day will be more gorgeous than any lace, crystal, satin, or hipster cummerbund.

Spreading the News

This is the last of the non-optionals. It's about getting the word out to everyone in your life about what's going on. The news you have to spread will depend on the choices you've made throughout the rest of this book. As you consider what you have to say, ask yourself:

- ❖ **Who?** Who is receiving your message?
- ❖ **What?** What do you have to say? What information do you need to impart? Keep in mind that there is objective information (date, time, place) and subjective information (mood, atmosphere, feeling)

The trick to getting your message across is to consider your audience's perspective. You know when you're watching a movie and suddenly you're looking through a character's eyes? That type of shot is called POV (point of view), and it's a compelling shortcut to understanding the character. Whatever it is you have to say, take a moment to put yourself in your audience's POV shot and consider how the message will be received.

IF YOU ARE HAVING A PARTY

Now we're in invitation land. Whoo-boy! Here's an opportunity to drop a wad of cash! Or not. If you start your invitation planning by Googling "wedding invitations" you may quickly come to the conclusion that half of your wedding budget will need to go to these little pieces of paper. Instead, let's start by thinking about the function of the invitations, and let form follow.

- ❖ **Who?** This is easy: your guest list.
- ❖ **What?** Well, to start with, there is the practical, tactical information:

Who's doing the inviting?

Usually corresponds to "who's paying?"

Who's getting married?

Date/Time

Place(s)

How to get there

How to respond, and what information you'll need

Anything from "Yes, I'm coming" to "I'm a vegetarian"

Other Info

One note here: I think (and it's just my personal opinion) that it's tacky to include gift registry information in an invitation. It implies some sort of tit-for-tat (I'm inviting you, so you have to buy me something) that isn't really appropriate. Here's what I suggest instead: Have an email prepared with a charming note and a link to your registry. Make sure your mom has it too, and shoot it off to *anyone who asks*. No one should get it unless they ask for it. Ok, I'll get off my soapbox now.

Now for the subjective information. You've put a lot of thought an effort into capturing a mood for your wedding, and letting that inform all aspects of the day. Think of your invitation as a hint of that, as your guests' first step into that world.

87

How can you fit your ambiance into a mailbox?

Use your colors, your mood, and your touchstone to guide your aesthetic choices.

Now, armed with this inspiration, you may decide not to shop for traditional invitations at all. You may opt to make something, or to go another route entirely. Or you may decide that engraved invitations that eat up half your budget are exactly what you need. The point is that the choice is up to you.

Save the Date

An optional touch, if you're inviting folks, is to send out a sort of pre-invitation. The idea behind this is that you should send out an informal invitation as soon as you've set your date (and you should never set your date until you've booked your place), so that your guests don't make other plans. Then, you send another more formal one at a specific interval of time prior to the wedding. And because, you know, engraved invitations take so long, so you need something to go out while you're waiting.

Is this necessary? Take a look at your schedule, budget, priorities, and the social calendars of your guests, and decide!

IF YOU'RE NOT HAVING A PARTY

Even if you're not having a party, there is still news to spread: you're married! That's a pretty big deal! How do you want to let people know?

The Who and What can get a little trickier here. A happy note or postcard may work for the vast majority of your acquaintanceship (see Announcement below), but you may have some delicate conversations ahead of you as well.

Even though I fully support it, your decision not to have a party may rub some people the wrong way. People like relatives who've been imagining your wedding since you were born.

Whether the news you have to impart is "We're getting married and we're not having a big party" or "We already got married, and we didn't have a big party" the key is to be really clear on your choices and reasons. Not that everyone is going to accept them; some folks may feel cheated out of a big event no matter what you say. But being clear on what the wedding means to you and why you made the choices you made will make your part of the conversation a smidge easier.

So... let's practice.

Why no party?

Take turns role-playing and practicing your answer.

Who needs the delicate approach?

Remember that you can practice what you want to say, but you won't know what they'll have to say, so you can't anticipate the entire conversation. As always, it's as important to listen as to talk during these conversations.

PARTY OR NO PARTY

Announcement

Whether you had a party or not, there were people you didn't invite. Do you want to spread the news to the rest of the world? This is part of your wedding, too, so your touchstone has everything to do with this choice too.

- ❖ **Who?** Who gets the news? Everyone you've ever known? Your 50 closest friends and relatives? Make a list.
- ❖ **What?** Whereas an invitation has a practical purpose, and announcement can say whatever you like. Make sure it doesn't read like a grab for presents, though.

What information do you need to share?

What feelings do you want to share?

GRATITUDE

Your wedding is all about the two of you, as it should be. You've just spent the better part of this book looking within yourselves and figuring out how to put your special stamp on your day. And because people who are excited and happy and in love are magnetic, the chances are that a lot of people have helped you out. Maybe they paid for part of the wedding, maybe they helped you schlep stuff, maybe they gave you their honest opinion about your choices, and maybe they gave you a set of salad tongs. Now it is time to turn your focus away from yourself and express your gratitude to these folks.

Timely thank you notes for wedding gifts are non-optional, but they're only a start. Take some time to consider everything that everyone else has put into this event, and how you can acknowledge those contributions. That doesn't have to mean spending a lot of money. It does mean sincerely expressing your gratitude: a meal, a speech, a phone call. In my experience, most people love to help, but they love to be thanked even more!

Name	What did they do/give?	How to say Thanks

Name	What did they do/give?	How to say Thanks

Name	What did they do/give?	How to say Thanks

Even if you opt for the smallest and most private of ceremonies, you do not live in a vacuum. Not only is a wedding big (and happy) news, but you'll now be facing the world as a married couple. This chapter is all about giving time and thought to the relationship between you as a couple and everyone else. I encourage you to share your feelings of joy and celebration. Chances are they'll be echoed back to you.

The Optionals

Remember "The List"? (Hint: it's on page 7.) I purposefully stripped the idea of a wedding down to its basics, to make it easier to think about. Well, we've covered all the non-optionals now. If you've been playing along, you should have a pretty good idea of what your wedding is all about. Now that the core of your wedding is in place, you get to have fun dressing it up.

So, do you want to see the optionals list? Here's a tiny sliver:

Attendants ❖ Attendants' gifts ❖ Band ❖ Bower ❖ Bridal shower ❖ Cake cutter/server ❖ Centerpieces ❖ Color Scheme ❖ Crab canapés ❖ Customized stationary ❖ Dancefloor ❖ DJ ❖ Doll with a miniature replica of your dress ❖ Favors ❖ Flower Girls ❖ Flowers ❖ Full bar ❖ Garter ❖ Gift registry ❖ Hairdresser ❖ Honeymoon ❖ Makeup artist ❖ Mini-busses (to ferry your guests around) ❖ Music ❖ Personalized vows ❖ Pouffy White Dress ❖ Professional Photography ❖ Printed cocktail napkins ❖ Programs ❖ Reception ❖ Rehearsal dinner ❖ Ringbearer ❖ Ring pillow ❖ Save the Date ❖ Sit-down Dinner ❖ Something borrowed, something blue (and a lucky sixpence for your shoe) ❖ Speeches ❖ Stag party ❖ Stretch limo ❖ Tent ❖ Toasting glasses ❖ Tossed rice/birdseed ❖ Tossing the bouquet ❖ Trees in the church ❖ Up-do ❖ Videographer ❖ Website

This is when you get to exercise all of your creativity on the bits and pieces that will really make your day sing. Remember the dreaming exercises back in the Touchstone chapter? Read over that again and pull out any details that jump out at you.

Write them down here:

Now close your eyes again. Knowing the choices you've made and the plans you've already set up, picture the whole day in your minds' eye, and fill in any missing details. What would delight your heart on this special day? What are you going to eat for breakfast? Is there anyone you want to say something special to? Are there any gifts you want to give out? What would make the day sing?

Extra Stuff   **What it means to you**

Pull out your touchstone and consider it. Not why you chose it or what you meant it to represent, but the actual image or words.

How can you bring your touchstone to life?

On my mantle, there's a photograph from our wedding. It's a wide shot—it shows about half the people who were there that day. Someone is giving a speech, and I'm throwing back my head in laughter, just like Isabella Rossellini in the photo that was stuck to my fridge. The bridge from touchstone to event may never be completely clear to you, but just stay focused on what you want to create. Your destination may not be exactly what you expect—remember, the trickster god loves weddings—but you'll get somewhere wonderful.

THINGS YOU DON'T NEED TO WORRY ABOUT (IN MY OPINION)

- ❖ Booking blocks of hotel rooms. Seriously, there are so many factors that go into travel plans—from "points" to allergies to phobias—that it's best left to the travelers themselves. Give folks plenty of advance warning, and let them feel great about their super-secret travel trick (everyone has one).

- ❖ Losing ten pounds. You're happy, you're in love, you're gorgeous. Remember to relax and be present, and you will positively glow. Besides, major weight fluctuations mean more fittings!

- ❖ Little Disposable Cameras. Don't even bother. They're expensive, and they are the perfect opportunity for a college buddy to rebut an old prank by taking an entire roll of people's feet (true story).

- ❖ Getting to your honeymoon immediately. By all means, tell everyone you're gone, but consider taking a couple of days for "down time" before you hop on a plane.

Afterword: Taking Care of You

Weddings have a way of taking over your life. And then, boom, they're over. Remember to tend to the rest of you through the weeks or months of planning.

List three things you love to do with your partner, that have nothing to do with the wedding.

A candlelit dinner, a walk through a farmer's market, a hike, a lazy Saturday morning in bed with a cross-word puzzle...

1)

2)

3)

Now book them on your calendar. This is non-negotiable time. And here's the trick: no wedding talk allowed. Do not let your candle-lit dinner turn into a project planning session. Do not spend your bubble-bath for two discussing whether Uncle Jerry should sit next to Aunt Jane. This is time for you to reconnect as a couple and remember why you're getting married in the first place.

List three things you love to do without your partner—with friends, family, or by yourself.

A mani/pedi, an afternoon in a museum, a baseball game, afternoon tea, yoga class...

1)

2)

3)

1)

2)

3)

Now book these on your calendars, too. Again, this is non-negotiable, non-wedding time. Do not attempt to decide on the color for the bridesmaids' dresses during Downward Facing Dog. Chat with your mom about *anything other* than the cost of an organic roast beef station. Take this time to reconnect with your passions in life and remember who you are. You'll still be that person after you've gone home married

Gratitude

First and foremost, thanks go to my husband, Alvaro, for never ever giving up on this book (even when it sat mouldering on my hard drive for years at a time). Thanks also to my most excellent proofreader, Stephen. And huge thanks and love to everyone who read an early draft and cheered me on.

Moi

I live near Washington, DC, with my husband and two gorgeous sons. I got married in Central Park, New York City, about two weeks after 9/11. Bypassers cheered.

My previous work includes "KnitSurfing the Subway" in *For the Love of Knitting* and "A Knitter's Therapy" in *Knitting Yarns and Spinning Tales*. I also edited the anthology *Knit It Together: Patterns and Inspiration for Knitting Circles*.

Yes, I knit. A lot.

Come hang out with me at **suzynjgonzalez.com**. I'd love to hear about your touchstone!

www.ingramcontent.com/pod-product-compliance
Lightning Source LLC
Chambersburg PA
CBHW070203290526
45789CB00002B/889